Contents

Acknowledgements

Without the help of the following people, this publication could not have been written:

Tim Arnold, WEA

Rebecca Avery, Kent County Council

Anthony Beale, Jisc RSC NW

Jon Farmer, Derbyshire County Council

Lisa Featherstone, Jisc TechDis

Phil Hardcastle, Jisc RSC East Midlands

Jim Hawkins, BBC Radio Shropshire

Scott Hibberson, Jisc RSC YH

Laura Higgins, UK Safer Internet Centre

Ruth Mable, DerbyLearn

Lorraine Maddock, Doncaster College

Mary Moss and Tezz, DAIN

Richard Nelson, Calderdale College

Jude Robinson, Art By Jude

Beth Snowden, Bradford College

Vashi Wood, CommonKnowledge

Foreword

The digital landscape has changed dramatically in the last decade and continues to develop rapidly. For many, it seems easier to ignore or avoid the risks of a life lived increasingly online through internet shopping and banking and online communities. However, the internet is a powerful resource in widening access to education, information and opportunity, and digital skills will be crucial if we want to participate fully in our communities, workplaces and economies in the future. An awareness of digital technology is now a necessity if we are to avoid a digital divide between those who are confident internet users and those who are not.

How do we balance the benefits of the internet with our concerns about the dangers of online interaction? It is important to understand enough to properly assess the real risks to learners, staff and organisations. There is a continuing need to raise awareness of the safety issues and to address the digital values, knowledge and skills that encourage us to behave responsibly online and enable us to keep ourselves and others safe wherever possible.

Although there is already plenty of advice for schools available, this guide presents the complex issues in context for the adult learning sector through relevant case studies and research that provide an insight into the digital issues that could have an impact on – or harm – a wide range of learners. Providers can consider a variety of approaches to e-safety and devise practical solutions and policies that are appropriate to the real risks they face. The guide offers support with the key steps in the process of implementing e-safety policies effectively and plays a part in promoting the digital literacy skills required for living, learning and working responsibly in an increasingly digital society.

Julia Taylor
e-learning advisor, e-safety
Jisc Regional Support Centre

Introduction

E-safety is an ever-growing concern for many people. The media are full of stories about the dangers of online sites and, in particular, social networking sites, an area where the rules of friendships and relationships are being re-defined. In November 2010, the media reported that a young mother from Bournemouth was terrified to find that a 'friend' she had added on Facebook was threatening to kill her new baby. She had added this person to the network (which allows you to add anyone you want to as friends, giving them access to your personal information and photos) because they had seemed supportive, but actually had no idea who they were or how she could get rid of them. In another high-profile case, a deputy headteacher who engaged in some risqué online banter with friends caught the eye of a local paper, resulting in a national scandal, suspension and her reputation being dragged through the mud.

However, the positive side of social networking is often missed out. Fifteen-year-old Leah from Kent didn't want to tell her teachers about a bullying incident, but found she could post about it using the non-face-to-face medium of Facebook where, spotted by local young people, she was given the support she needed. Jude, an adult feeling isolated due to her spinal problems, was able to access a supportive community and eventually start her own business, thanks to Twitter.

Indeed, despite the scare stories, studies are increasingly showing that giving learners of all ages access to online sites is not only sensible but also beneficial, provided that safeguards are put in place and responsible practice is observed. Digital advocates are increasingly suggesting professional use of these networks as well, resulting in dilemmas for many not just in the teaching and learning sector, but also in the medical, care and public office professions, as conflicts between personal and professional online identities explode. An increased focus on safeguarding from Ofsted, the inspectorate for adult education in England, together with an emerging focus on digital literacy and the expectations of learners and, in some cases, their parents or guardians, have left many education providers wondering which way to turn.

This book aims to act as a guide through the minefield of e-safety, examining:

● why people might use, or benefit from, online interaction;

● what the dangers of online interaction might be;

● what guidance already exists on the subject; and

● approaches for taking the issue forward with learners and staff.

It is worth noting that some of the issues covered here may not be comfortable reading. While this book won't go into any kind of detail, it is inevitable that some of the subject matter may upset some people. It is also important to be aware that this book does not, in any way, constitute any kind of authority on legal matters and the reporting of studies and guidance are very much the author's own. While parts of this book will make reference to particular platforms, the aim is to provide a broad guide that will stand the test of time in a rapidly changing environment; after all, safety is often about common sense, reasonable precautions and a measured – not reactive – response.

This book is not intended as a definitive reference on the subject of e-safety, nor as an in-depth manual for advanced practitioners or technical experts. Instead, it aims to broadly outline the issues involved, the guidance available and the approaches that can be used to integrate e-safety into a curriculum.

Part 1
Why e-safety matters

In order to understand e-safety, one first has to understand why it matters. In much the same way as with broader health and safety issues, there is often disagreement about the levels and severity of potential danger, the need for preventative action and the nature of the protections put in place. This part of the book looks at why e-safety is an emerging issue, what the debates surrounding it are and, more importantly, what the dangers are.

The connected society

Tezz had left university due to financial troubles and was struggling to find work. Looking online, he came across a local digital inclusion project called the Digital Activist Inclusion Network (DAIN), where he became a volunteer. Concerned that many of the elderly people he came across were socially excluded, he wanted to teach them the benefits of connectivity and show them how Skype could be used to keep in touch with people. He watched one person get in touch with their family in Germany: 'It was really moving to watch their face light up and you feel proud for being able to help them', he said.

Jude found herself unable to leave her home in the countryside, so she turned to social media for support. 'Twitter and Facebook became my lifeline', she says, 'and the friends I made online were a great support to me when I started becoming an artist. It meant that what was meant to be a hobby became a successful business. Twitter particularly is a place to gain support on a personal level, to ask questions and to open up interesting discussions'.

These case studies, and the many others around the country that echo them, show just how relevant communications technologies are, not just to young people but right across the age, gender, skill and financial spectrums. Such technologies are, in essence, a form of learning in their own right and are certainly key in widening participation and empowering disadvantaged learners. Connectivity is rapidly becoming part of everyday life and many day-to-day tasks are now primarily online, along with thousands of commercial services that allow us to book holidays, buy books and groceries, and even order a takeaway from our computers, tablet devices or smartphones.

Connectivity has spread to the classroom too. Increasingly, learners are downloading, copying and sometimes creating online content, and some are using Facebook or similar platforms to connect with their tutor. In several local authorities, adult tutors use Facebook as a communication tool, informing learners of everything from upcoming deadlines to when a session is unavoidably cancelled. This is backed up by statistics from an Ipsus Mori/BBC poll[1] indicating that 49% of young people

---

[1] Ipsos MORI/BBC (2012) *Media Literacies: Understanding Digital Capabilities*. At: http://downloads.bbc.co.uk/learning/learningoverview/bbcmedialiteracy_26072012.pdf Q14a (accessed 04/09/2012).

coming online for the first time were drawn there to find support with their learning.

However, connections are not just taking place in the classroom. More and more, industry is encouraging workers to connect, both for their own and their companies' benefit.

This increasingly connected society brings with it great benefits for efficiencies, collaboration and change. Of course, it also brings with it a new set of dangers which apply to novice and advanced users alike.

E-safety, safeguarding and e-responsibility

E-safety is often seen as a subject for children and young people. It is argued that adults, broadly speaking, do not need safeguarding as they are old enough to make their own decisions. Adults are not vulnerable to grooming because they are in a position to consent to any relationships they may choose. As a result, many e-safety organisations concentrate their resources on young people and those adults they class as 'vulnerable'.

The reality, however, is that with a technology this new, everyone is at least a little vulnerable. Irresponsible use of the internet can leave individuals, companies or even large groups of people exposed to dangers, which may not be a matter for safeguarding authorities but is important when it comes to the welfare and life skills of learners.

That's why many in the adult learning field are starting to use the term 'e-responsibility' instead – the concept is about using the internet (or other online platforms) responsibly rather than being about using it safely.

Digital literacy

Digital literacy is key to ensuring that people of all ages can use and benefit from online activities safely and responsibly. The concept has been around for a number of years (the popular CLAIT course stood for 'computer literacy and information technology') and, until recently, was seen as a fluency in software and tasks used in the work environment, such as word processors or spreadsheets. Increasingly, however, it is being adapted to refer to online skills, not so much as skills that are additional to literacy and numeracy, but rather as ones that are essential for day-to-day life.

Jisc Advance recently set up a programme to look at digital literacy in further education (FE) and skills, and defined digital literacy as being:

> **'... those capabilities which fit an individual for living, learning and working in a digital society: for example, the skills to use digital tools to undertake academic research, writing and critical thinking; as part of personal development planning; and as a way of showcasing achievements'.**

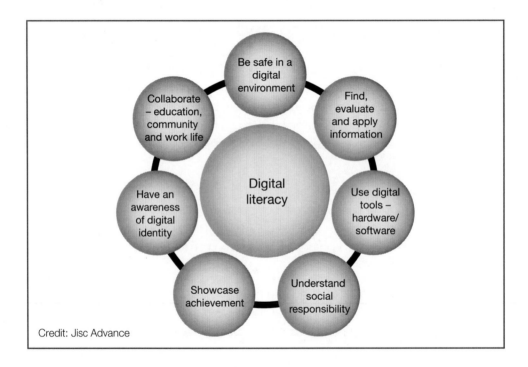

Credit: Jisc Advance

Part of digital literacy is the understanding of **digital identity**. This can mean not only the footprint you leave online when using social networking sites, but also the data that is made available about you on the public record (e.g. the electoral roll or Companies House data) and data that is tracked from sources as diverse as store cards or energy meters.

Learners

Many adults assume that young people are 'digital natives' who naturally understand the way the internet works and, as a result, are literate in using it. However, this model is increasingly argued against by FE college staff who realise that many of the learners they work with are using the internet frequently but are still not clued up about the tools available, information-seeking skills or the safety precautions needed. David White from Oxford University rejects the idea of digital natives and, instead, refers to those who are frequent and seasoned online users as 'residents' and those who use it occasionally as 'visitors'.[2] Some digital residents may struggle to understand the implications of the tools that surround them, despite being able to use the technology. This is backed up by Ipsos Mori/BBC research,[3] which found that confident adult web users rated security as moderately difficult, while younger users generally struggled more with understanding the safety implications.

Staff

While there is a rapidly increasing number of tutors and education leaders with basic or, indeed, expert digital literacy skills, the fact remains that many staff have no concept of the set of tools known as Web 2.0 (applications with interactive elements), social media or collaborative technology. There are good reasons why staff may want to avoid social technology – but it is equally true that staff with no skills in using it run the risk of isolating themselves from learners who base much of their life around it. What is more, there is an increasing level of expectation that staff have a responsibility to guide learners. In addition to the inspectorate requirements detailed in this book, there is the vital task of responding to learner need: 21% of adults said that if they wanted to know how to undertake a new task on the web, they would ask a colleague or teacher, and the figure was higher still with younger learners.[4]

For these reasons, digital literacy should be seen as an across-the-board issue, applying equally to learners and staff of all ages and apparent computer usage skills.

Types of danger

When digital literacy is low or ineffectively applied, or when strategic monitors and preventions are misapplied or not in place, then, like any other avenue in life, mistakes

---

[2] White, D. (2008) Tall Blog. At: http://tallblog.conted.ox.ac.uk/index.php/2008/07/23/not-natives-immigrants-but-visitors-residents/ (accessed 05/09/2012).
[3] See 1.
[4] See 1.

occur and people are left vulnerable. There are two different approaches to looking at the dangers posed, as discussed on the following pages.

Individual/institutional/infrastructure

When the term e-safety is mentioned, perhaps because of the safeguarding issues, the danger is always assumed to be one of child abuse, grooming and identity theft. But, in fact, digital harm can be caused in many different ways and it is often the less obvious ways that prove to be the most dangerous, simply because they had not been considered.

There are three types of harm, known as 'The Three I's'.

- **Individual**. For most people, this is the most serious type of harm. It's when you as an individual are harmed, either physically, mentally or professionally. Bullying, abuse and damage to your personal or professional credibility are all examples of this and most of the negative press that online platforms get centres around these issues. In terms of adult learning, individual harm can apply to learners, staff or indeed anyone associated with the learning experience. Harm can also come to you in terms of your personal data (which could include information based on where your mobile phone was as much as information you've entered into a database) if this is illegally or unethically stored, used or abused.

- **Institutional**. Harm isn't just done to people on an individual basis. Reputational harm to organisations can occur when legitimate complaints are badly handled in an online environment, when malicious rumours spread 'virally' (that is, they spread quickly and beyond the control of the originator), or when deliberate online hate campaigns are started.

- **Infrastructure**. This occurs when a technical system is taken down, for example by a computer virus (a programme that maliciously damages a computer or network) or a denial of service attack (a method used by hackers that involves bombarding a website with information until it stops working). At worst, this can permanently destroy expensive systems on which people depend; however, it is more likely to disable them for a time, incurring a large cost, rather than endangering lives.

These categories need not be exclusive; for example, if a member of staff uses an online chat room to torment a pupil, this could damage both an individual and the reputation of the institution. Online hate campaigns, particularly by large-scale protest groups, may well include attacks on infrastructure. Indeed, infrastructure attacks don't always leave computers disabled. They may, instead, leave computers or networks vulnerable, meaning that institutional or personal data can be harvested by individuals for whatever purpose.

Contact/content/conduct

In order to clear up some of the ambiguity around what constitutes danger online, many e-protection organisations now use 'The Three C's' as a method of categorising dangers:

- **Contact**. These are dangers that learners face due to inappropriate contacts. This could mean those who groom, those who bully or those who try and steal personal, financial or identification information.

- **Conduct**. These are dangers that have consequences for the perpetrator, resulting from their irresponsible use of the internet to express prejudice or endanger their personal reputation by, for example, sharing compromising photos publically.

- **Content**. This is intentional or unintentional exposure to dangerous content. This could include sites that incite crimes or damaging behaviour (e.g. self harm), or it could include overly sexualised or illegal images.

Some organisations have also added a 'fourth C', while others put this under Content:

- **Commercialisation**. Uploading, distributing or downloading items that are protected by copyright or other intellectual property laws.

The 'Three I's' or 'Three C's' systems serve as useful guidelines when looking at approaches to tackling e-safety, which we'll explore in the next part of the book. Before we can get there, however, it's important to consider some of the dangers in more individual terms. This is one section of this book that will quickly go out of date – as soon as one danger is tackled, another rears its head. The list on the following pages, however, provides a brief sample of some of the dangers identified at the time of going to press. It's worth reading them even if you are familiar with e-safety, as there may be ones mentioned you've not heard of before.

As detailed in this book, the same technology that is of great benefit to society can be the same technology that presents a danger. When reading the list, it is worth remembering that many of the platforms mentioned have also been used for positive effect and forbidding or blocking the use of them may be unnecessary or counterproductive. Nevertheless, it is important that we consider how, when applied in a negative way, useful platforms can also present dangers to learners of all ages.

Potential safety issues

Creep photos: Photos that are often compromising and always taken and uploaded without the subject's knowledge or consent, sometimes to sites specialising in such content or to social networks.

Criminal content: Criminal content will normally incite or depict crimes (for example, bomb-making guides or photos of sexual abuse). Coming across such content may upset viewers or cause them long-term harm. Definitions can be found at www.iwf. org.uk/hotline/the-laws

Cyber bullying: The concept of bullying via online media. This can take the form of traditional bullying (i.e. name-calling, rumour-spreading (called 'cyber pesting') and harassment) or it can take a specific online form. Examples of the latter could include impersonating a person via a website or social media profile, asking them embarrassing questions on sites that allow anonymous questioning of the account holders, or by hijacking their online accounts and posting compromising or humiliating content appearing to be from them. In many cases, much of this is illegal.

Cyber stalking: Using someone's digital footprint to track where they are, possibly for illegal or malicious reasons. Sites that contain the electoral roll, use street-level photographic maps, or apps and networks used by people to show their location also make this possible. Those registered as company directors or who are involved in public office are sometimes surprised to find that their details are available online.

Digital identity/footprint: The data that is stored electronically about us, possibly without our knowledge. This may be data that we choose to upload (e.g. for social networking purposes) or that is collected by others (for example, via store cards, energy meters, etc.). There are growing concerns that profiles constructed from data gathered about individuals, coupled with content they post to social networking and other online sites, could be used to predict behaviour for commercial or criminal gains.

Fraping: 'Facebook raping'. An uncomfortable term used to describe the malicious accessing of another person's social media account, often by using a device like a smartphone where a user is permanently signed into a social network, and deliberately updating the status or uploading photos that humiliate the victim (e.g. 'Kevin is picking his nose right now', though usually less tame than that). This is illegal in many circumstances.

Geolocation: These are games and tools that use a smartphone's GPS (similar to a sat nav) to pinpoint their exact location for use online. For example, it might map the photo to the point it was taken or might allow users to find friends or recommended businesses nearby. In the case of some sites, it might broadcast their exact location (to within a few metres). These can all be useful and, in case of keeping track of loved ones, even have safety benefits if used correctly. However, misuse (for example, pinpointing your home address to the public) can be a danger. It's worth noting that some applications post data without asking consent every time (or occasionally without asking at all), so someone sending a message who was unfamiliar with the initial setup might be surprised to find out that their exact location was attached to the public message they had sent.

Grooming: The act of someone (usually an elder) persuading a victim (usually a minor) to trust them, before using that trust to gain personal gratification (often in the form of sexual abuse of the victim). Groomers do not always try to meet their victims, but may ask them to perform acts in front of a webcam, share compromising personal details or engage in inappropriate conversation, sometimes recording the details for personal gratification or in order to blackmail the victim as their next attack. This is illegal and taken very seriously by law enforcement authorities.

Hate sites: Sites set up deliberately to attack an individual or group. They may take the form of direct threats, ridicule and humiliation, accusations and rumours or as a spoof of a real profile. Some may (usually illegally) encourage action against an individual or group.

Litigation: Increasingly, people who use the internet to express views, share information or criticise individuals, groups or organisations in an illegal way (e.g. race hate, libel or contempt of court) are finding themselves in legal trouble. While it may seem obvious that illegal speech would have legal implications, many people think of their Twitter feed as 'pub banter' and don't consider the public implications of what they say.

Obscene content: Obscene content can be pictorial or written. There have been a number of arrests relating to obscene content (often posted by trolls or cyber bullies) and the Crown Prosecution Service has posted guidance on this, which can be found at www.cps.gov.uk/consultations/social_media_consultation.html.

Messaging services: Secure and encrypted text messaging systems, such as those used on secure smartphones, have often come under criticism for providing criminals, particularly those involved in violent disorder and terror plots, with a platform for communication that is not easily intercepted by security or law enforcement agencies. The systems normally provide the facility to send to multiple devices at once without the originator being easily traceable. These systems can be advantageous for people engaged in spreading unfounded rumours, hate campaigns and cyber bullying activities.

Münchausen by internet: While not a recognised disorder, this term was coined by psychiatrist Dr Marc Feldman[5] to describe people seeking sympathy and attention by faking illnesses online. Although it is not a widespread problem, it is normally particularly traumatic for the victims who have supported people with supposed illnesses and conditions, only to find they never had one in the first place or, worse still, have scammed the victim out of money.

Phishing: A method of stealing personal data by having a website that pretends to be a different site; for example, a website that looks identical to your bank website. However, when you enter your account details and password the site stores it elsewhere, normally for the purposes of stealing your identity or financial security details.

Pro-ana: A term used to describe content on the web which seeks to legitimise, encourage or even incite anorexia. Despite a perception that pro-ana websites promote harm, it is more common to find 'thinspiration' content on social networking sites, in particular those that promote the sharing of pictures, often via mobile devices. Other self-harm sites and content include pro-suicide, pro-drugs and pro-self-mutilation, again often taking the form of social media content, though occasionally existing as static websites. A recent study suggested that some of these networks may, however, provide support to those with eating disorders or other conditions.

Revenge porn: Sites that contain (often sexual) images of people that the individuals would not want others to see. The site normally names the individuals concerned and often links to social media channels or websites associated with that individual. This content is sometimes uploaded by cyberbullies or others with malicious intent and sometimes obtained through 'fusking', a process for automatically retrieving images from photo sites. Fusking may obtain photos that the originator thought were protected from public view.

Sexting: The sending of sexually explicit or suggestive content (normally self-taken images or video, but also suggestive texts) via text message, instant message or over social networks. This act is often illegal when minors are involved and can cause great distress to the victim if the images are accidentally or maliciously shared with others. This is primarily an issue for young people; however, adults sharing images should also be aware of the dangers of them falling into the wrong hands. The Association of Chief Police Officers has provided guidance for young people concerned about the

---

[5] Feldman M. (2000) *Münchausen by Internet: Detecting Factitious Illness and Crisis on the Internet*, http://demo.ort.org.il/clickit2/files/forums/920455712/634495323.pdf (accessed 05/09/2012).

legal implications of sexting, with a view to ensuring that those who fall victim are not afraid of the legal ramifications of reporting the incident. This can be found at: www.ceop.police.uk/Documents/ceopdocs/externaldocs/ACPO_Lead_position_on_ Self_Taken_Images.pdf

Trolling: A troll is someone who intentionally causes upset in an internet discussion. While a 'flamer' may intentionally post controversial views in order to stimulate a heated debate, a troll deliberately upsets, normally off-topic. The worst examples include those who go onto memorial websites, forums and social networking pages and intentionally parody a person's death or their perceived lifestyle prior to death, or verbally attack the victim's friends or families. A troll may also be a cyber bully who contacts individual people to upset them by posting cruel, abusive or threatening remarks. This is sometimes illegal and, increasingly, police are taking this matter very seriously.

Webchat sites: These allow users to chat privately, normally with video, to random strangers who are also using the site. If a user dislikes the content they can report it or click one button to move to another stranger. The chat model promises a chance to meet new people but has been accused of leading to sexually inappropriate conversations or, in the case of video, illegal sexually graphic content. Criminal elements are known to use these sites to gather images.

Summary

● E-safety and e-responsibility are important to all learners and staff, irrespective of whether they use much online media and their skill (digital literacy) level.

● Responsible use of online technologies is part of digital literacy, which is increasingly being seen as a life skill.

● There are many dangers that people may not be aware of, even if they are experienced web users.

Part 2
Approaches as a provider

In Part 1 we looked at why e-safety was important. It's easy to read that section and decide that, in fact, social media and online learning is so riddled with danger that it's best to just avoid the whole thing. If that's what you're thinking, no one could blame you.

However, Part 2 seeks to turn that notion on its head – not only are there real positives to online learning and social networking, but it may be dangerous to ignore it altogether.

In order to discover these positives in a safe environment, it's important to consider the situation carefully, evaluating how to approach it. This part of the book guides you through the steps that you as a provider can take to ensure that your systems, together with your leadership and management, are up to the task of dealing with e-safety.

Four approaches to e-safety

When it comes to the e-safety issues, there are four possible approaches that you could adopt. All four are currently in use in different schools, colleges, councils and other providers around the country. They are as follows:

1. **The 'shut eye' approach**. This approach is the easiest and, in the short term, the least costly. If you adopt this approach you simply say: 'That's never going to happen to me', close your eyes and do nothing at all. Hopefully, in this case nothing will occur and, in many situations, it won't. If, however, it did, the lack of safeguards might mean it was more serious and you'd have few grounds on which to defend yourself, having not put safeguards in place. This approach is often the realm of the small organisation that thinks it knows its learners well, the person who doesn't use online tools themselves so sees no personal danger from them or the libertarian who believes that e-safety is simply 'common sense'. Ultimately, all of those may be right; however, that would provide little comfort to an abused learner, nor would it pay the mortgage for a disgraced teacher or institution. What's more, Ofsted does not appear to favour this approach either.

2. **The 'lockdown' approach.** For many providers, in particular those working in local authorities, this will be the approach currently being used. The theory is simple: if people can't access these tools, they will be safe (see, however, 'The risk of not' below). Lockdowns can be done in various ways. Some organisations lock down all sites, allowing only the ones they approve through (called white-listing). Others 'black-list' (block) the sites they don't want people to access. Yet others limit access only on certain computers (for example, some colleges allow social networking on social computers, but not in the library). The latter example might be considered part of the measured approach.

3. **The 'measured' approach.** This is a hybrid of the 'lockdown' and 'shut eye' approaches, which seeks to allow experimentation in a controlled environment. For example, one local authority has opened up access to all social networking for staff while evaluating whether it has a positive or negative impact on productivity and customer services. Many businesses now open social networks during lunch hours and colleges are designating certain computers as 'social computers'. Others block social networking on college-owned machines but allow it over WiFi so that students can use it on their own devices. This method only really works in tandem with the 'guidance' approach outlined below.

4. **The 'guidance' approach.** This method is favoured by many academics and inspectors. It suggests that learners should be guided through the areas of e-safety, not by blocking sites in their entirety but by providing a safe and supported environment in which to learn about e-safety. This approach is very reliant on systems being in place to provide that safety. One downside of this model is that those giving the guidance, often teachers and tutors, need to have high levels of digital literacy. A way of tackling this may be to use peer mentors.

The risk of not

When drawing up risk assessments it is very easy to get pulled into a negative spiral of 'what happens if...?' What happens if someone is groomed? What happens if someone uploads illegal material? It's right to have these concerns and the process of risk assessment requires that you consider them all. However, one risk that is rarely considered is 'the risk of not'. What is the risk of this person **not** using social media? What is the risk of learners **not** being able to access the sites they need to? What is the risk of teachers and tutors **not** being able to enhance teaching and learning or deliver it more effectively simply because something is blocked? Ultimately and, as we will see in the next part of this book, with good grounding, we must ask whether learners are more at risk by **not** having access to online platforms. These risks need to be taken into account and seriously considered. There are always balances to be made. For example, in a college situation, it might be decided that the risks to learning and to individuals are too great if personal smart phones are permitted in the classroom; however, the use of them in social areas is fine.

Becta's PIES model

In looking at approaches to e-safety, the now closed education technology agency Becta developed the 'PIES' model. PIES stands for **P**olicy & Procedure, **I**nfrastructure, **E**ducation and Training underpinned by **S**tandards and inspection. The model suggests a guidance approach (i.e. education and training around e-safety) but one that is clearly backed up with sound policy and procedure and technical infrastructure settings (e.g. blocking, monitoring, etc.) when required. All this is underpinned by the requirements of Ofsted.

Studies and guidance

There are an increasing number of studies that suggest that the guidance/PIES approaches are not only preferable, but essential for learner wellbeing. While this book does not cover in-depth critical analysis of the literature available on the subject, some of it has been summarised below. It's important to note that all of the studies focused on pre-18 year olds. While some of the findings will no doubt have similarities with adult counterparts, there is currently no research to substantiate this.

These studies focus primarily on the issue of e-safety itself. Those with an interest in the subject may additionally want to look at the broader issues that e-safety raises; for example, there are many studies on how digitally collected data can be used to profile the lifestyle choices and habits of individuals, the ethics of providing platforms for social interaction or the nature of the online world in terms of combating or re-enforcing social isolation. In addition, many organisations and professional associations have developed firm policies on the issue of e-safety which have given rise to extensive academic debate.

The Byron review

The most well known guidance on e-safety in the UK is that produced by Dr Tanya Byron in 2008 under government commission.[6] It found that the internet 'offered a range of opportunities for... learning and development' and that 'young people need to be empowered to keep themselves safe'. It criticised the model that online and offline concerns are the same, summarising: 'While internet risks can reflect offline concerns, the problems can be qualitatively different and sometimes have the potential to be more damaging'.

The report suggested that monitoring tools could help 'manage access' – but they only worked when correctly understood – and the need for learners to be educated and build resilience to material was also important.

The report was very detailed when it came to family learning, making a specific recommendation that education be developed to 'improve the skills of children and their parents around e-safety'. It also recommended that e-safety form an essential and embedded part of the curriculum, not just for students but also for teachers entering the profession. It said that action needed to be taken 'at a whole school level', pointing to the Becta guidance on the subject (see previously).

---

[6] Byron, T. (2008, 2010) www.education.gov.uk/ukccis/about/a0076277/the-byron-reviews.

Importantly, it also said that those who work with children and young people should have an 'appropriate understanding' of e-safety to help support and protect children online, calling for a 'culture of responsibility' between parents, children and teachers.

The report was followed in 2010 by a review which, amongst much praise for the pace of change, suggested that teaching should be further developed to allow children to 'manage the digital space positively and safely'.

The EU Kids Online study

The most comprehensive study on e-safety was carried out by the EU Kids Online Network in 2011.[7] Led by Prof. Sonia Livingstone from the London School of Economics, the study worked face to face with 25,142 children aged 9–16 and their parents in over 25 EU countries.

The detail from this report is extensive; however, some key findings were as follows:

● Going online was now 'thoroughly embedded' in children's lives.

● Online risk (i.e. the chance of children finding something adults might feel is disturbing) was considerably higher than the chance of online harm (i.e. the likelihood of them actually being disturbed or harmed by something/someone they found online).

● Allowing children to experiment with issues and identity, while 'risky', was also 'vital' for them to develop adult coping mechanisms.

● Children who take risks offline are also more likely to take risks online, though it was also found that those who took fewer risks were more likely to be upset/harmed by the content they did come across online.

● Importantly, the report found that upskilling young people meant they took more risks; however, they also explored more opportunities. The study argued that this was a good thing, providing they were not exposed to content that went beyond their ability to cope. Those with fewer skills were more likely to experience harm from the same content. Cyberbullying was, by far, the most harmful content children encountered and, while more skills might mean they were more likely to encounter that harm, they would also be better equipped to cope with it.

● Children who experienced upset would tell a friend or family before they told a teacher, despite the teacher being, arguably, best equipped to help.

[7] Livingstone, S. *et al.* (2011) *EU Kids Online*, www2.lse.ac.uk/media@lse/research/EUKidsOnline/
EU%20Kids%20II%20(2009-11)/EUKidsOnlineIIReports/Final%20report.pdf (accessed October 2012).

- Due to the use of mobile devices for web access (around 33%) it was better advice to work with children on internet risks than to make them use a 'family computer' where they could be supervised.

- Children from economically disadvantaged backgrounds were found to be more at risk from harm than those from more advantageous backgrounds.

The study recommended that educators should be:

- up to date with technology and resources and should take 'major responsibility for supporting children and their parents in gaining digital literacy';

- looking at ways of 'harness[ing] the potential of peer mentoring'; and

- considering e-safety as a 'core dimension' of the curriculum.

The University of Illinois study

The research undertaken by Prof. Brendesha Tynes in 2007[8] may now be dated (it refers to the 'new' phenomenon of YouTube); however, it still contains some very important points that echo other studies. It found that:

- informal training in 'critical thinking and argumentation skills' through social media can be effective;

- those living in racially segregated areas were able to meet people from differing communities, suggesting that 'peer learning that takes place across racial and ethnic boundaries' could be 'more effective than educating from textbooks because [they] construct learning for themselves';

- teenagers 'can and do' seek online advice before making a decision and this can 'provide them with a space to try out and enhance their decision-making ability'; and

- if blocked from accessing the internet, young people will find alternative ways to access it anyway.

The research suggested the following key strategies:

1. Maintain open and honest dialogue between teachers, parents and teenagers.

2. Help young people protect their privacy online.

---

[8] Tynes, B.M. (2007) 'Internet safety gone wild: Sacrificing the educational and psychosocial benefits of online social environments, *Journal of Adolescent Research*, vol. 22, no. 6, pp. 575–584, http://jar.sagepub.com/content/22/6/575. abstract (accessed October 2012).

3. Help young people develop an 'exit strategy' for when online spaces become harmful, whether that involves blocking, reporting or simply ceasing to partake in a harmful activity.

Ofsted guidance

Rightly or wrongly, the primary concern for many providers when it comes to e-safety is the implications of e-safety on the Ofsted inspection. At the time of writing, there has been much political discussion around Ofsted and its role, including in e-safety. As a result, this information is subject to change, though correct at the time of writing.

In its handbook for inspecting further education and skills, Ofsted makes no specific reference to e-safety. It does, however, make reference to the importance of safeguarding procedures, support for learners and skills such as 'taking responsibility'. Additionally, briefings by Ofsted further education and skills inspectors have indicated that e-safety is to be taken seriously. To ensure that providers comply, it is worth noting their guidance for pre-16 inspections. While some of this might not apply in post-16 education, it is important that post-16 educators consider the same issues. For example, many schools use The SHARP System (School Help Advice Reporting Page) as a platform for the reporting of e-safety related incidents. This may or may not be suitable for an adult learning institution, but the importance of having clear reporting mechanisms remains the same, with only the method of reporting changing.

In 2012, Ofsted's guidance on 'Inspecting e-safety' included the following as examples of good practice:

● a whole-school, consistent approach

● robust and integrated reporting routines

● staff

● policies

● education

● infrastructure

● monitoring and evaluation.

Within this it is very clear that there should be rewards for positive and responsible internet use. Many providers really struggle with this area, so here are some tips for encouraging learners.

Tips for encouraging positive behaviour

✔ Use online learner voice forums to get learner feedback, then respond and action where possible.

✔ Use role play or other innovative ideas to explore e-safety and digital footprint scenarios.

✔ Set safe tasks associated with online activity (for example, research a safety topic on Wikipedia).

✔ Get students to design their own e-safety contract. In design-based courses, this could be done as a visual warning poster.

In addition, Ofsted's guidance says that the following would be inadequate:

● a lack of 'planned and progressive' (i.e. not 'one assembly per year') training on e-safety;

● students not understanding the reporting mechanism;

● a lack of evidence of staff training; and

● a lack of any filtering or monitoring.

Ofsted notes that a strategy should not be 'generic', suggesting that it wants to see something that works, encourages participation and leads to a safer environment for learners, rather than just a strategy that makes information available. The guidelines include some sample questions for leadership and management and pupils. They deal mainly with the theme of ensuring that systems are in place to educate students and that there is an 'exit strategy' for them to report and see actions on dangers.

Putting together a policy or strategy

A starting point

The first step in putting together a strategy and policy is to review where you are. This is a hard thing to do on your own, however it's important to get started. The first thing to do is to see if you can answer 'yes' to the following questions:

- Do we, as a provider, have a clear e-safety policy that is separate to our Acceptable Use Policies (AUPs), bullying policies, etc? (Note: Don't re-invent the wheel – the e-safety policy can be a separate entity, but should link in with existing policies, rather than repeat them.)

- Do I, as a member of staff, know what the safeguarding procedure is in terms of e-safety-related incidents or concerns?

- Do we, as a provider, have a team of people who are responsible for e-safety, whether as part of the broader ICT or the safeguarding strategies, or (preferably) as a separate venture?

If the answer to any of these is 'no' or 'don't know' then you need to follow the steps below.

Putting together a team

The exact makeup of an e-safety team will vary depending on the type of provider and its size. It can't be stressed enough that the founding and makeup of this team is crucial not only to the development of the strategy, but also to the effectiveness of the safeguarding system. It is common in busy teaching environments for management to delegate positions on e-safety teams to junior staff; however, this is to be strongly discouraged. It is important that e-safety is viewed as part of the management team's responsibility, as some changes will require approval and resources. Who exactly makes up the e-safety team could be open to negotiation; however, as an absolute minimum it should include the following:

- **Someone from the senior management team.** This could be the principal, a Head of Service (HoS) or an assistant principal/HoS with responsibilities in this area.

- **The safeguarding officer.** This is the person who is responsible for implementing the safeguarding of student policies.

- **The person ultimately accountable for safeguarding.** Usually, this is one of the above. However, if it isn't, they need to be included.

- **Someone senior representing ICT.** The reason this person needs to be senior is that they need to be able to make, or at least influence, decisions around blocking and infrastructure security.

- **Someone representing curriculum staff.** Obviously it is important to have staff input into the practicalities of any policy, and staff will also be able to suggest methodologies for embedding e-safety into the learner and CPD curricula.

Those are the essentials. However, you may well want to, and indeed should, include some of the following people too:

- **Someone representing learners.** The learner should be central to any institutional policy and they can have some very strong opinions on e-safety issues; plenty of colleges report that they block some social media specifically on the learner's request. Learners are also likely to be aware of current trends in internet media, so their feedback may be valuable.

- **The Head of the LRC/ICT suite.** If you are a provider that has an LRC or an open-access ICT suite, it's useful to have a representative on board. In several FE colleges, this is the person who is appointed responsible for e-safety. If you are a local authority provider that makes strong use of public libraries, someone from public libraries might be a good start.

- **Communications officer.** This is very important if you are considering institutional damage or the way staff communicate using social media. Don't underestimate the importance of organisational reputation in e-responsibility or social media strategies.

- **HR/trade union officer.** If you are likely to be drawing up policies around staff use of social media, particularly if the policy is going to include conduct outside of work (which it often should), it is useful to have this/these officer(s) on hand.

- **Pastoral staff.** It's important to target e-safety provision for vulnerable groups and pastoral staff will play an important part in identifying these learners and supporting them in accessing the curriculum in a safe and positive way.

Now that you have a team, it's time to revisit your review process.

Reviewing where you are

There are several tools available for doing this. Publically funded post-16 providers in the UK can access a service helping them to benchmark their e-safety provision from their local Jisc Regional Support Centre. The service also provides a link to wider resources at: www.jiscrsc.ac.uk/esafety.aspx.

In addition, there is a series of comprehensive resources provided by the South West Grid for Learning. The Online Compass (www.onlinecompass.org.uk) is a set of free e-safety resources for organisations that work with children and young people outside of schools. Designed for community groups and similar organisations, it helps not just with benchmarking but also tracking your progress. It is sister to the 360° Safe (www.360safe.org.uk) self-evaluation tool, which is designed for schools and, like the Online Compass, can be completed online or downloaded as an offline tool.

The outputs from these tools are far more comprehensive than can be summarised here; however, the following five questions should be top of your list:

1. Do we have a workable policy and procedure that all staff and all learners are aware of in terms of:
   a. reporting issues of abuse, bullying or any other online misdemeanour, whether internally or to relevant authorities;
   b. use of social media by staff and learners in a variety of contexts; and
   c. use of provider-owned ICT systems and learners' own devices?

2. Does this policy encourage and reward safe online behaviour?

3. Does this policy link with existing policies (e.g. bullying, AUP, etc.)?

4. Do we have parameters in place to know these systems work?

5. Are we confident that we are doing all we can to ensure our learners are safe, not only in learning time but also in the wider world?

Proofing your policy (loopholes)

When considering a policy, think about its flexibility. If it is not workable, it will be ignored and become ineffective. So, if you state: 'Learners may not use their own devices in college and notices will be put up to this effect', students will probably ignore the message. If you say: 'Learners may not use their own devices in the classroom; however, they may use them in the social area where posters about safe use will be displayed', your policy is likely to be more respected and will probably be more effective.

The more absolutes you put in, the more you risk policies being rejected. Here are some key ideas to avoid:

- Staff may not use social media (what, ever? What about on their own devices and in their own time?)

- Staff may not add students as friends on social networking sites (see 'Behaviour and communications')

- Mobile devices can never be used in the classroom (not even if they help learning?)

- Staff and/or students are not permitted to discuss the provider on social media (how would you police this? What can people say and not say?)

E-safety is a very individualised subject, so the following headings should be taken as guidance only in developing your policy.

Under these headings, there are various references to other policies (e.g. data protection) – again, this should not re-invent the wheel, just link to existing policies as required.

Statement of policy and intent

This section needs to look at why you are drawing up the policy and who it will be going to and needs to clarify the providers' intention and commitments with regards to online platforms (e.g. does the college recognise that mobile phones play a part in learning, or do they feel that they have no place in the building?)

Roles and responsibilities

In this section, you lay out the specific roles of individuals and groups. These might include the roles of following:

- the e-safety team (and possibly an e-safety officer)
- senior staff
- teaching staff
- other staff
- mentors (if you have them)
- learners
- parents, guardians or carers if appropriate.

It is important that the roles and responsibilities assigned to people within your provider are considered. Here are some issues you may want to think about:

- **Overload of small issues.** Will you get lots of reports of 'he called me a **** on Facebook', taking away time from the serious issues like abuse? However petty these issues may sound, they will not be petty to the learners involved and they will need responding to. Can responsibility be split between different people?

- **Approachability.** Often, the person ultimately responsible for e-safety is a director or principal. How confident would staff and learners feel about approaching this person with an issue, and would they be easy to contact?

- **Cover.** If specific people are named in the policy, what is in place to ensure their role is covered in case of absence or if they leave? A generic phone number or email address, shared by a team, might be an approach to get round this provided that appropriate procedures are in place to ensure that it is checked regularly.

Bradford College needed to put in place an e-safety strategy.

Their first step was to contact relevant agencies that could help, including their local e-safety partnership, LSIS and Jisc RSCs.

They used the offline version of the 360° Safe tool to evaluate their position. After this they put together a competition for students to design posters promoting e-safety. The winners' posters were then used throughout the college, including being turned into mousemats, not only to raise awareness of e-safety, but also to act as a positive way of reinforcing safe and responsible behaviour.

Security

This part of the policy looks at the infrastructure part of e-safety (see the 'Potential safety issues' and 'BECTA's PIES model' sections). It should not just be around blocking unsuitable content, however, but should also take into account phishing, identity theft, the security of the IT network and data protection.

In addition, this section might cover the relationship between the e-safety policy and the Acceptable Use Policy (AUP). The AUP is seen by many as the grounding for the e-safety policy – but this is not always the best idea. An AUP is a contract between a user and the person who owns the system they are using, not a statement of safeguarding, so needs to be appropriately supported and developed. However, the two policies should certainly work hand in hand. The responsible and safe use of provider-owned ICT systems, and possibly the provider's WiFi connection, are governed by the AUP. Additionally, the AUP needs to make reference to where safety procedures can be found. As the AUP is normally presented to and read by staff and learners at induction, it is important to consider whether the e-safety policy should be distributed this way too and, if not, whether the AUP should reference it, with the wider e-safety policy expanding on the detail. What the AUP should not cover as a policy in itself, however, are the following:

- issues around staff contact with learners over social media;

- issues with staff and learner use of online platforms when not accessing them through the provider's system; and

- issues around bullying which does not take place over the provider's own system.

The reason that these don't belong in an AUP is that they are bigger than the institutional system that the AUP governs. However, they should still be addressed, so the need for a wider e-safety policy is paramount.

Furthermore, the security section of the policy should consider the implications of learners using their own devices – this might be particularly important when working in outreach situations with low/no connectivity. It is also important to consider the implications of providers giving WiFi access. There is much debate around legal guidance for learners' use of their own technology, so it is worth taking legal advice on this.

Behaviour and communications

This section examines the issues around conduct online and how students and staff communicate using online tools. It should, within the reasonable and acceptable scope of a policy, reference both providers' and learners' own devices and their use in and outside learning time.

Students can and will use social media to collaborate around college, in both a positive and negative way. This policy section may wish to consider:

- what content is deemed unacceptable and the consequences of using it; and

- procedures for dealing fairly with any criticism of the provider and/or staff that is posted online.

Social media use by staff is probably the subject for another book, although it is still worth touching on the subject here. How staff behave on social media sites in and out of work can affect both their personal and professional reputations and this can bring the institution or profession into disrepute. Some of the issues to consider are:

- the posting of embarrassing, compromising or offensive pictures or content;

- the posting of, or allegiance to (e.g. joining a Facebook group or retweeting), opinions that go against corporate values or conflict with codes of conduct and contractual arrangements, particularly in terms of equality, diversity and accessibility; and

- the posting of content related to work, colleagues, students or the workplace.

You may want to consider having a separate social media policy to cover this area.

The relationship between staff and students on social media is a tricky dilemma, but needs to be covered in the behaviour and communications section. There is a fear, backed up by a small but significant amount of evidence, that tutors befriending students will leave the teacher wide open to judgement, ridicule or, worse still, accusations of grooming or other offences.

It must be remembered that, particularly in adult learning, teachers and students may have a relationship prior to their professional one and also that some teachers may wish to forge relationships in order to build on social media as a communications tool, or to keep in touch with student progression. If the policy is not flexible enough to accommodate this, teachers may befriend students 'under the radar', undermining the policy completely and exposing both sides to potential dangers.

Many teachers and tutors get round this by having two profiles, one personal and one professional. This is against the terms and conditions of several networks (most notably Facebook – it's worth reminding learners and staff to examine these terms, rather than just accept them) and still leaves staff open to allegations arising from private communications. It also means teachers may see postings on a student's site about sensitive subjects (such as substance abuse) and feel the need to act. This is good safeguarding practice, but can seriously compromise a professional relationship.

Other teachers will not want to add students to their social network at all which is, of course, fine; however, if they use publicly available social media, they will need to know how to manage their privacy settings so that their content is not available to browsing students or members of the public or press.

As a result, here are some options:

- Staff who wish to use Facebook can set up a Facebook page or a Facebook group either for themselves or for their department or group. A page does not reveal the personal account to the students, and allows for interaction without access to personal details, but pages are public and can be 'liked' by others so confidentiality will still need to be considered. Appropriate procedures should be in place (e.g. risk assessments, management approval and AUPs) to establish clear boundaries for use.

- Staff can add students and use privacy settings to filter content that is suitable or unsuitable for students but it is highly advisable that the policy ensures that line managers are made aware of these instances to ensure transparency, protecting both the learner and the member of staff.

- The policy could discourage social media friendships between staff and learners, but suggest that, where a case can be made for the friendship to exist (e.g. a pre-existing relationship), details are registered with a line manager.

This section should also make a statement around internet monitoring and whether or not the provider will actively monitor content.

Use of image, video and personal information

This section of the policy should focus on the use and storage of content on student- and staff-owned devices and what is acceptable to record and distribute. For example, can a student film a session? If so, who do they need to get permission from? Can a teacher take photos on their own device and thereby keep ownership of them beyond the provider's control?

Many providers also have policies around the storage of personal data. This should not be prohibitive; for example, there may be times when it is acceptable to store soft content (e.g. lesson plans) on the cloud, or harder data (e.g. personal details) on institutionally controlled servers; however, procedure should be based on legal advice and in line with the data protection policy and law. In terms of safeguarding, it must protect learners and staff from dangers arising from the accidental loss or distribution of personal data. This section may also want to consider data transmitted about students that could be used to develop a profile of their online or offline behaviour.

Education and training

This section covers how the policy will be cascaded to staff and learners.

There is normally some reluctance from both; in the case of staff, they often don't see how e-safety is relevant to them (especially if they don't use social media themselves) and, in the case of learners, they often feel that they already know the issues. Neither of these situations is normally true. Here are some approaches you might want to consider:

- using learner/staff inductions (sometimes video based), online courses (see the DerbyLearn case study) or formal training slots;

- using scenarios and role-playing games to illustrate the subject (Jisc Regional Support Centres have developed resources for doing this); or

- relating the e-safety issues to real issues that learners may come across and asking them how they would deal with these.

In this section, it may be worth considering what areas you wish to cover with learners. For example, safety and security using social networking is commonly seen as the foundation for e-safety; however, digital data footprints, information skills for validating online content and the downloading of copyrighted or protected works are other crucial issues that may need to be addressed.

DerbyLearn decided that the best approach to e-safety education was to have a course in their learning platform, Moodle. Working with the Jisc Regional Support Centre East Midlands, they developed a course which linked to relevant materials that all staff and students could work through at their convenience. This course covered the dangers, positive aspects and approaches surrounding e-safety and links to further resources.

They embedded this module in every course delivered, regardless of curriculum area, and developed an additional one for learners with disabilities.

Incident, response, feedback and monitoring

Your policy is only as good as its functionality and, as discussed in the Ofsted section, how you monitor its effectiveness is essential. Here are some tips for this:

- Design a flow chart of the reporting system so it's clear who is responsible for what.

- Ensure procedures are developed for situations when it is important to involve outside agencies (e.g. dealing with criminal behaviour, allegations against staff and vulnerable learners). These agencies will normally include the police or, in the case of young learners, the Child Exploitation and Online Protection Centre (CEOP), and the local authority designated officer for child protection (LADO).

- Display information posters throughout the building (see the Doncaster College case study).

- Ensure that you have a method of recording each instance of a report and any actions taken, even if reports come from a variety of different avenues.

- Ensure that you gather feedback on resolution outcome, the time taken and the satisfaction with that outcome.

● Regularly ask students and staff if they are aware of the procedure and where to find it, pointing them in the right direction if not.

Appendices

It's worth including documents that may illustrate the policy here, as well as links to useful organisations. Many are included in our 'Useful links' section (including a helpline for any member of staff who is unsure what to do). Flow charts of reporting and responsibility may help familiarise the process.

Doncaster College wanted to get the e-safety message out, so they printed a series of posters, business cards and mousemats. These were placed around college but, in particular, in open access ICT centres and the learning resource centre. Their text, rather than containing much detail, urged readers to 'tell someone' if they felt upset and gave them a web link to a site where students could report any concerns or find further advice.

Summary

- You need a policy and strategy that is flexible and measured, not prescriptive and restrictive.

- Your policy should be put together and reviewed by a team.

- Clear lines of responsibility should be drawn up, illustrated and disseminated to learners and staff.

Part 3
Approaches with learners

Having a policy, strategy, resources and materials are worth nothing if learners themselves are not engaged with the subject of e-safety. As many have learned the hard way, engaging them can be an uphill struggle. Many learners either feel they know it all or are so turned off by technology that they don't see it as applicable to them. In this final part, we'll examine some of the core issues that all learners need to know, provide some practical examples of how to introduce them and explore how some providers are working with niche groups to introduce e-safety in areas where it may not previously have been addressed.

Providing an exit route

The 'Report It' button

As well as knowing the procedures, it's important that students always have 'an exit route' as detailed in several of the studies mentioned. The following are two possible approaches to this:

- the use of a pre-made button, such as the CEOP 'Report It' button; or

- the use of a provider page which gives reporting options, including links to the CEOP button.

A provider page gives the students the chance to report non-illegal behaviour and approach the college before the police, where appropriate.

The CEOP button should be displayed prominently on all provider websites, on any virtual learning environments and on any social media groups or pages. Before using the button, it's worth considering its purpose and effectiveness. CEOP are very much engaged with the protection of children who are being exploited, often online. As a result, reporting instances of cyber bullying, identity theft or defamation would not be effective for either the reporter or for CEOP operatives. That said, if someone vulnerable, in particular a child, does need swift and sound protection, the CEOP button is by far the most effective tool available.

It is also important that people know how to report and self-police their social networking. You may have a peer system for self policing or students may want to use the 'report' button found on most interactive websites. They should bear in mind, however, that reporting things takes time and that many social networks will only remove posts or pages if they violate their terms of use; in many cases, what a learner might feel is offensive might not be covered in the network's terms and conditions.

 Richard Nelson, an ICT lecturer at Calderdale College, set up a social network site using the platform 'ning'. The students were keen to self-police the site and did so. At one point, a student interested in rap culture uploaded some pictures of guns. This resulted in an enthusiastic online discussion from students about the ethics of the images and why they made some students uncomfortable. As a result, the student voluntarily removed them without a need for any staff involvement or disciplinary action.

How do learners communicate?

Many learners will not use telephone calls or even email as their primary method of communication. Social networking and text messaging are often preferred methods and, unsurprisingly, are where learners might often feel most at risk. It may, therefore, be worth considering whether the provider could instigate reporting methods that work through social media, text messaging or QR codes, which can be scanned from a phone to provide links to websites and email addresses.

E-responsibility in the curriculum

E-responsibility need not be a session in itself and can be broadly integrated into the curriculum. Many subjects lend themselves to examining the importance of aspects of e-safety; for example:

- photography, media and art classes can examine issues of intellectual property rights, subject to consent;

- any subject using research can evaluate the validation of online information (information literacy);

- any subject dealing with data (such as maths, numeracy and sciences) can examine the storage of data; and

- any subject with a philosophical element (e.g. sociology or psychology) can debate the ethics of implied consent, privacy, online versus offline personas, etc.

Promoting an e-safe culture

An e-safe and e-responsible culture is important both within and outside the learning institution. Your policy and strategy should cover the internal areas, including ensuring that everyone is clear on reporting procedures and, more importantly, is confident in approaching the appropriate people in order to make disclosures.

However, promoting a culture outside of the institution is often much harder. A good approach to this is to encourage students to explore the subject themselves and share best practice. Social bookmarking sites are ideal for this, as resources can be easily indexed and updated. One example of this is the Digital Literacy Diigo group maintained by Jisc Regional Support Centres (https://groups.diigo.com/group/digital-literacy-jisc) and the ScoopIt's that Jisc staff maintain on the subject (www.scoop.it/t/e-safety and www.scoop.it/t/digital-literacy-education).

In the case of some social bookmarking sites, learners could tag additional content, adding to the information.

Keeping informed

It's worth noting that the assumption that learners know more than you on the subject of e-safety is rarely accurate. While it is almost certain that they will know about some sites that you don't know about, you may equally have knowledge of others and, if you are not digitally confident yourself, you will be approaching the subject with an impartial point of view; sometimes it's easy for someone who doesn't use social media daily to see the error in an activity that an active user takes for granted.

What is important is that you stay as informed as possible. Organisations such as The UK Safer Internet Centre (www.saferinternet.org.uk) maintain newsletters, and advisory services such as Jisc Legal, Jisc Tech-Dis and Jisc Regional Support Centres can provide excellent advice on up-to-date issues. Social media sites such as Twitter and blogs by e-safety experts are other key ways to stay up to date.

Working with niche groups

Talking about 'vulnerable learners' in this context is nonsense as most learners are vulnerable to at least some of the pitfalls of the emerging issue of e-safety. However, those working with niche groups may require specific examples.

Jisc Legal, in a publication covering specialist colleges, note that all e-safety resources must be in a format accessible to all, or could be in breach of equality laws.[9]

Digital isolation

Around 16% of the UK population are still not online and many do not have access to a reliable connection due to rurality or other issues. These learners will find e-safety a particularly daunting prospect and digital literacy, as defined earlier, will be of primary concern. It may be that specific courses around digital literacy will aid these learners.

---

[9] www.jisclegal.ac.uk/Portals/12/Specialist%20Colleges%20Law%20and%20ICT.pdf

E-safety in secure settings

Tees, Esk & Wear Valleys NHS Foundation Trust have done work around e-safety with learners in a secure forensic mental health unit. All their learners were patients who were detained under sections of the Mental Health Act.

The Trust introduced access to the internet on a small number of machines. Access to patients was granted following a risk assessment on a one-to-one basis. These assessments were designed to control the risks rather than to prevent access. For example, one patient had previously been guilty of harassment via the internet. As a result, the patient was only allowed to use email under one-to-one supervision, although was able to use other parts of the internet without issue. Social media remained blocked in the unit, however, and online e-safety courses were used to prepare patients for the world of social media, email and other e-safety issues upon being discharged. Sessions that needed to be tailored to a more specific level or to a specific area of e-safety were delivered by staff and also embedded in functional skills sessions. The method has been pioneered in the forensic unit but is in the process of being rolled out across the trust, which means that e-safety work will take place with mental health inpatients on general wards and services specific to dealing with eating disorders and to adults with learning difficulties.

E-safety for people with learning disabilities

CommonKnowledge is a Glasgow-based charity that produces accessible online learning for people with learning difficulties. Much of the charity's work has been around creating a specific, safe, social network for people with learning difficulties. Finding very few resources around e-safety and learning disabilities, but recognising a growing concern around people with learning difficulties using mainstream social networks, they created resources around the issues of cyber bullying, hate crime (CK Respect) and meeting someone online (CK Sex Talk). These resources were designed to be as inclusive as possible, using graphics and speech readers. The charity is currently working on a peer education project to train older learners with learning difficulties to support others.

E-safety for carers

Derbyshire County Council feels that those working as carers have a distinct need to learn more about e-safety. They have implemented a course specifically aimed at those involved in fostering, adoption or residential care.

Updating it annually, they now offer a guidance document for free download and regular training events. They specifically focus on confidentiality and privacy, in relation to caring responsibilities.

E-safety for family learning

There are increasing examples of e-safety being taught in family learning situations that suggest that parents and carers learning alongside their children promotes not only safer families, but also increased engagement of adult take-up of the subject.

Summary

- Many learners will require specific support around e-safety.

- Learners need to be aware of internal and external methods of reporting offensive content.

- Learners needs access to an 'exit strategy' if they ever feel they are at risk of harm.

Conclusions

E-safety and e-responsibility are complex issues that merit a great deal more research and discussion. There are no simple answers and their developing nature means that everyone from the digitally excluded to the security expert has skills to learn for the future, whatever their age or perceived level of vulnerability. Learning institutions, be they large schools or informal adult learning providers, will need to remain at the forefront of this for the foreseeable future, so putting policies in place now is not only a priority; it's essential.

Useful links

Internet Watch Foundation
www.iwf.org.uk
For reporting images of child sex abuse and finding out more on the laws around illegal content.

Child Exploitation and Online Protection Centre (CEOP)
http://ceop.police.uk
For reporting any instances or suspicions of online child sex abuse.

UK Safer Internet Centre
www.saferinternet.org.uk
Latest advice on using the internet and new technologies safely and responsibly. Includes a helpline 0844 381 4772 or helpline@saferinternet.org.uk for professionals working with children or young people who have e-safety concerns.

Jisc Regional Support Centres
www.jiscrsc.ac.uk/esafety
Support for most post-16 education providers in setting up an e-safety strategy.

Jisc TechDis
www.jisctechdis.ac.uk/techdis/userneeds/esafety
E-safety resource for independent specialist colleges.

Jisc Legal
www.jisclegal.ac.uk/themes/esafety.aspx
Support around the law and e-safety in further education and skills.